Michaël Borremans

Michaël Borremans
The Acrobat

With a text by Katya Tylevich

David Zwirner Books

A Sermon at the Circus: Michaël Borremans Chants the Profound from a Trapeze

With his paintings shipped overseas for the exhibition *The Acrobat*, and his studio in Ghent suddenly empty, Michaël Borremans paces the room, refusing to turn on a light as the sun sets outside. "I hate it when lights are on during the day," he says. "I'm very sensitive to light." Shadows are important to his work, he admits, but light is an irritant. Perhaps the artist simply doesn't like to see his studio empty. The scent of oil paint coats the air. The presence of those paintings may be felt there forever.

"I remember being six or seven years old, going to church and staring at the paintings of saints. I couldn't keep my eyes off them, thinking, How could someone have made this? I knew I wanted to make it, too," says Borremans. "Painting is an old medium. It has so much gravity, it makes its subjects sacred."

The potential for humiliating and degrading the human body is vast and comical. Death itself is nothing special, but a truly gruesome act demands originality. Contemporary examples are nothing novel, built as they are on history's burial ground. The martyrs and saints, subject to innovation, fill its graves with their tongues cut out and breasts lopped off, legs broken, fingernails mutilated, and, of course, nerves punctured by nails.

Today's obedient churchgoer or ecclesiastical tourist, however, gazing at portrayals of suffering in a Renaissance altarpiece, rarely sees disfiguration, even if there is some blood. Icons stare past the nave in beatific shell shock, and painted bodies appear hearty and stuffed. The decent act of the liturgical artist would be to weigh the eyelids down with pennies and let the dead rest. But even the most famous crucifixion scenes evoke resurrection and not rigor mortis. The artist plays the role of embalmer, rather than coroner, denying the appearance of death though staring directly at it.

Like a body, "a painting is always on the verge of collapse," says Borremans. In his work, the artist alludes to breakdowns—societal, psychic, and cellular. He keeps the breaks from materializing. Among Borremans's painted references are execution hoods, body bags, the stress positions of tortured bodies, the regalia of terror and the occult, clans, worship and ritual, the superstitious, the violent, the inert, and the indifferent. The artist takes images that we otherwise view between our fingers and makes them easy to see. *Easy* on the eyes. Upright on the cross, and well fed on the chapel ceiling.

In Jan van Eyck's 1432 Ghent Altarpiece, the sacrificial lamb—the titular protagonist of the central panel, *Adoration of the Mystic Lamb*—should be a carcass, collapsed. Instead, the lamb bleeds neatly from its mortal wound and remains standing, staring, taxidermic. Since its completion, the altarpiece has been stolen and damaged at least seven times. It was, most recently, kidnapped and held hostage by Nazi footmen, as per Hitler's attribution of supernatural powers to the artwork. Recovered and narrowly saved from destruction, the altarpiece now spends its days in a constant state of restoration and artistic pampering: its depiction of the dead and sacrificed is so mystical and enduring that the object itself is constantly being resuscitated, resurrected, and given a fresh powder of rouge.

In the fifteenth century, van Eyck seduced with an aura of transcendence. He used the novelty of oil paint to drill the depths of human strangeness, picking at the seams of convention to betray his figures' emotional contradictions. In the twenty-first century, Borremans does analogous things. He plays with human posturing, both in the literal and the metaphoric sense. He props the limp upright, heats up cold bodies, and will not accept his figures' letters of resignation. His oeuvre jokes about civility and hints at depravity. "I do not paint fact and I do not paint portraits," says Borremans. He paints, in one sense, contradictions.

To describe Borremans's masterworks, a riff on Jan van Eyck is gorgeously unoriginal. Borremans anticipates the lineage in which critics and historians will place him, then sends those comparisons down a rabbit hole. In a neat model of the evolution of art, Borremans's work is a mutant in a five-piece suit: an evasive omnivore that devours van Eyck with as much pleasure as it does Man Ray, Luis Buñuel, and Francis Bacon. The beast eats the sacred and the impious; it stalks the mundane and the strange. Borremans creates a generational synthesis in his work. The argument between patience and mania in his brushstrokes is a séance with Diego Velázquez, while the sudden and hilarious veneration of a mechanical appliance, such as in *Apparatus (II)* (2017), is a challenge to Marcel Duchamp for a duel.

The artist communicates a confusion of time through an absence of chronological markers and through costume and clothing. Many of his subjects wear absurd or embarrassing outfits. Some wear threatening allegories, others dress in the trappings of polite society, all buttoned-up and ironed flat. These figures, hushed and unprovocative, could be the vernacular of 1930s Europe, the advertisements of 1950s America, or snapshots of reserved contemporary society, with its appalled members clucking their tongues but minding their business.

Borremans prompts the viewer to look over one shoulder at the past. Meanwhile, his work's magnetism pulls the viewer forward. The viewer rips in two, becomes of two minds, begins to dissociate, disintegrate, doubt, and, most important, feel.

The work is reflective and ponderous as it scans the newspaper for war crimes. It time travels and teases with visions of what might be. It is science fiction and fantasy, but also documentary B-roll of current brutalities and boring dinnertime small talk. Borremans conjures memories of loved ones whose hearts have stopped beating. It's all there in the work: The waiting. The ventilator being deactivated and the breath ceasing. Borremans paints the vacuum. He likewise sends flowers and tongue-tied condolences. The wake. The mourner bends over the casket and has little of importance to say.

In the aerial view of Borremans's works, there appear to be two types of bodies: those on display and those of the onlookers. They are the hostages and the hostage takers. The artist withholds any obvious sympathy toward either but more readily positions the viewer as one of the onlookers. The viewer, all dressed up and tight-lipped, is a ticketed visitor to a distinguished colosseum for that afternoon's bloodbath. The artist hopes you enjoy the show.

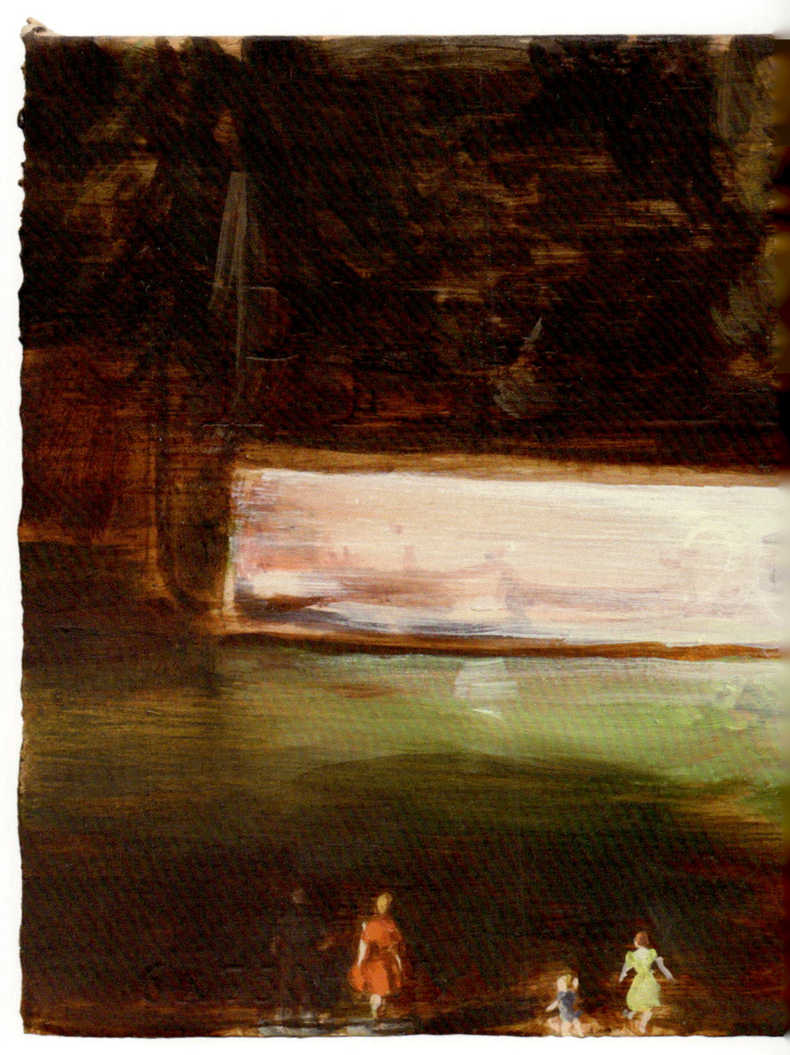

10   *Milk (or The Acrobat) (Design for a Sculpture)*, 2021

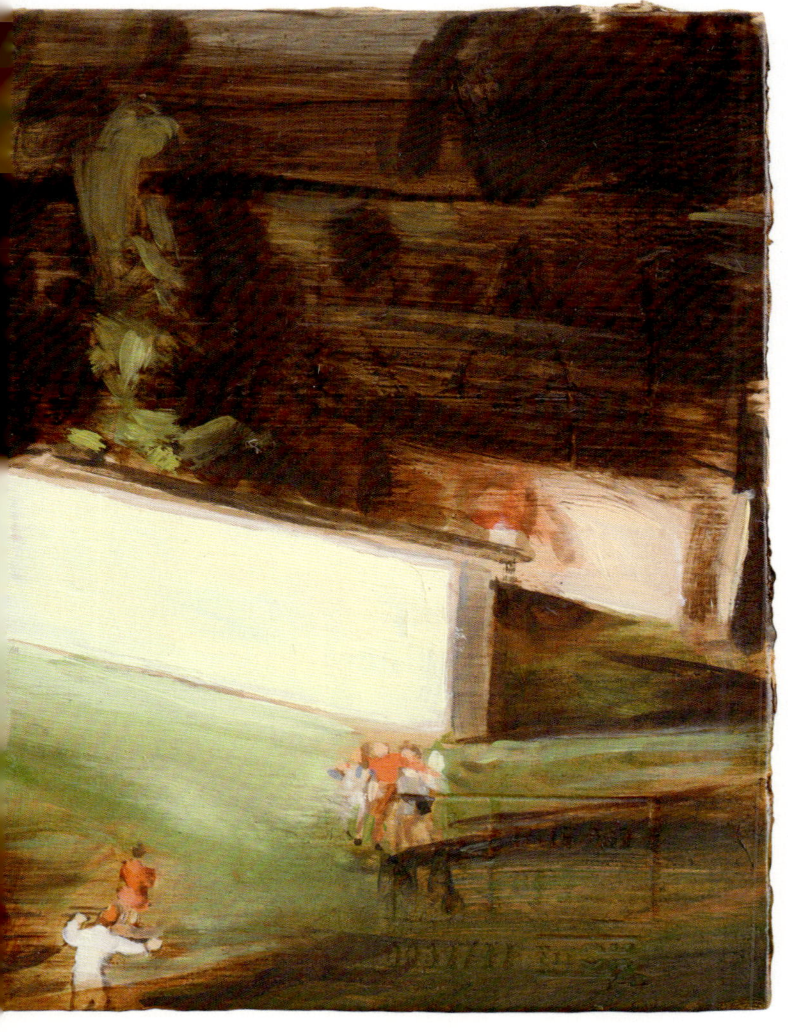

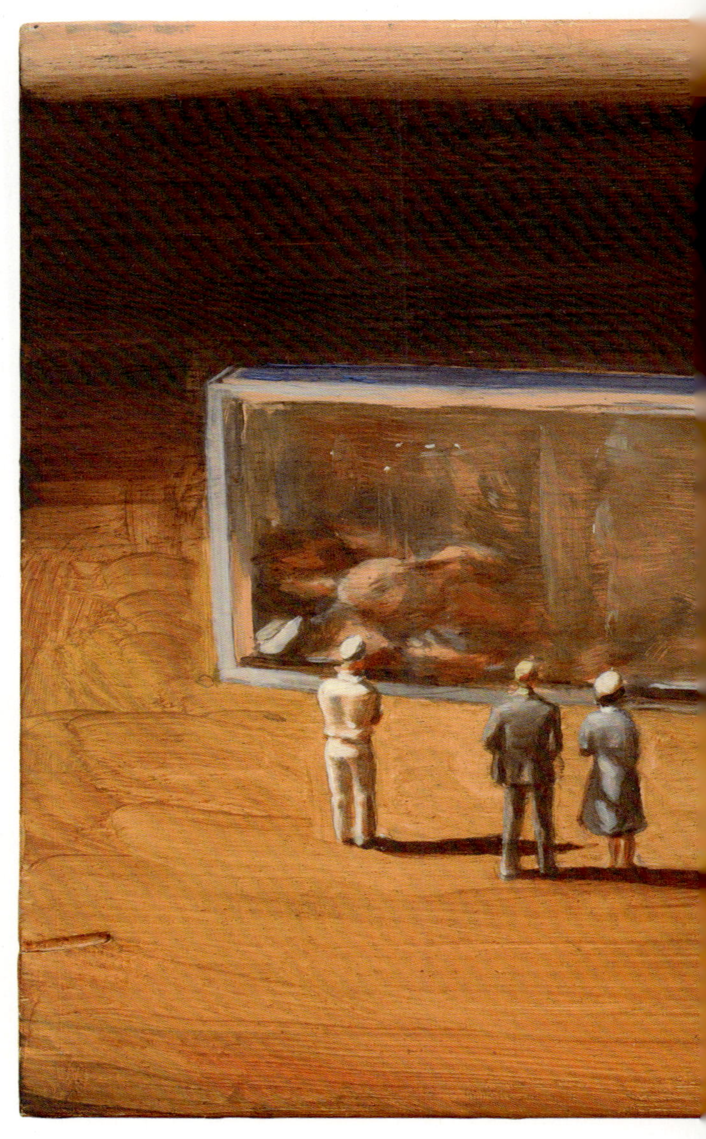

12   *With Animals*, 2021

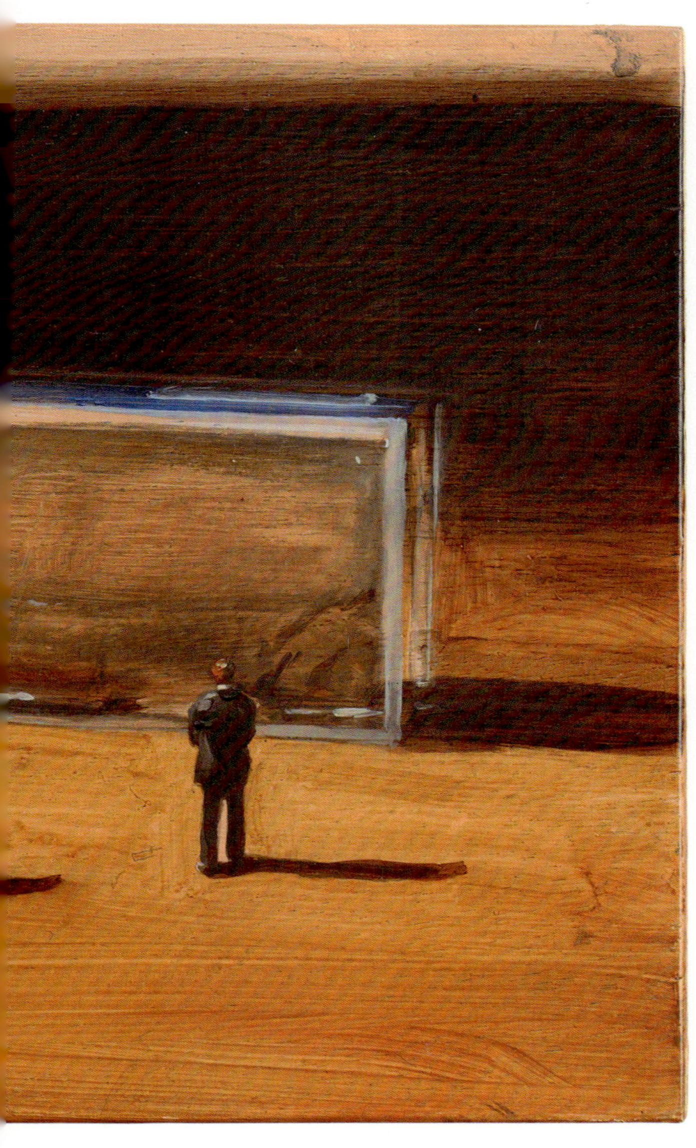

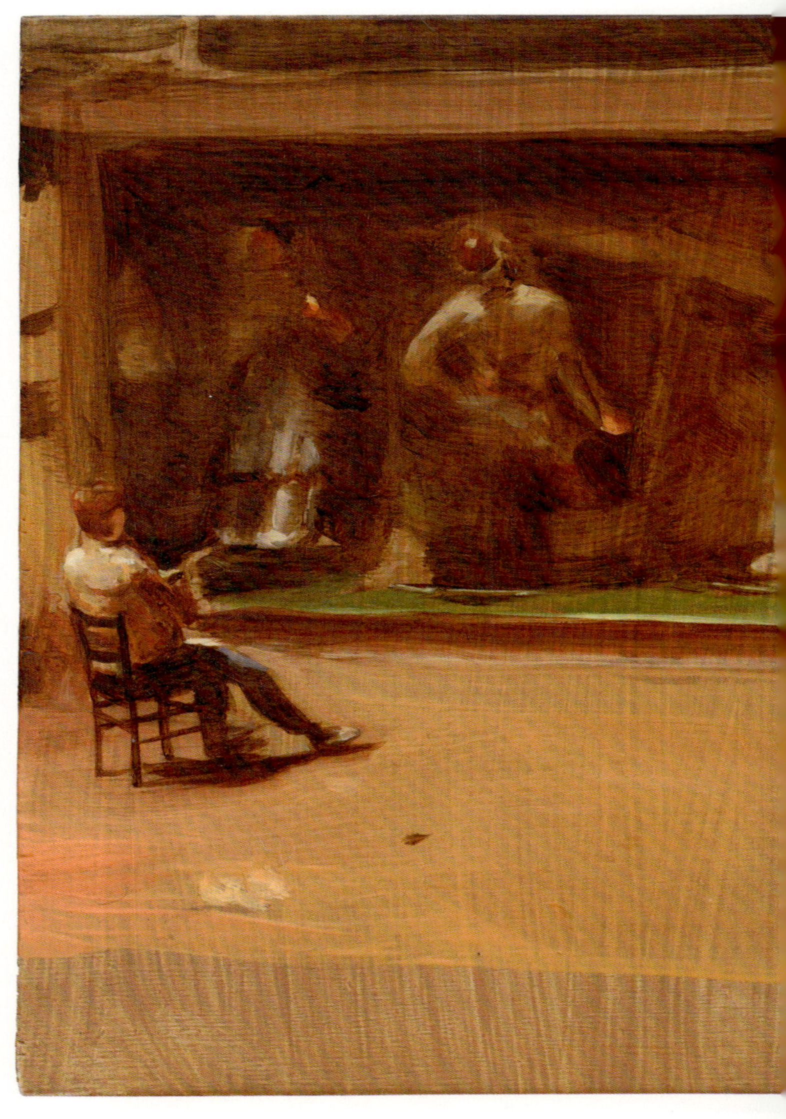

     The Fog (Design for a Sculpture), 2021

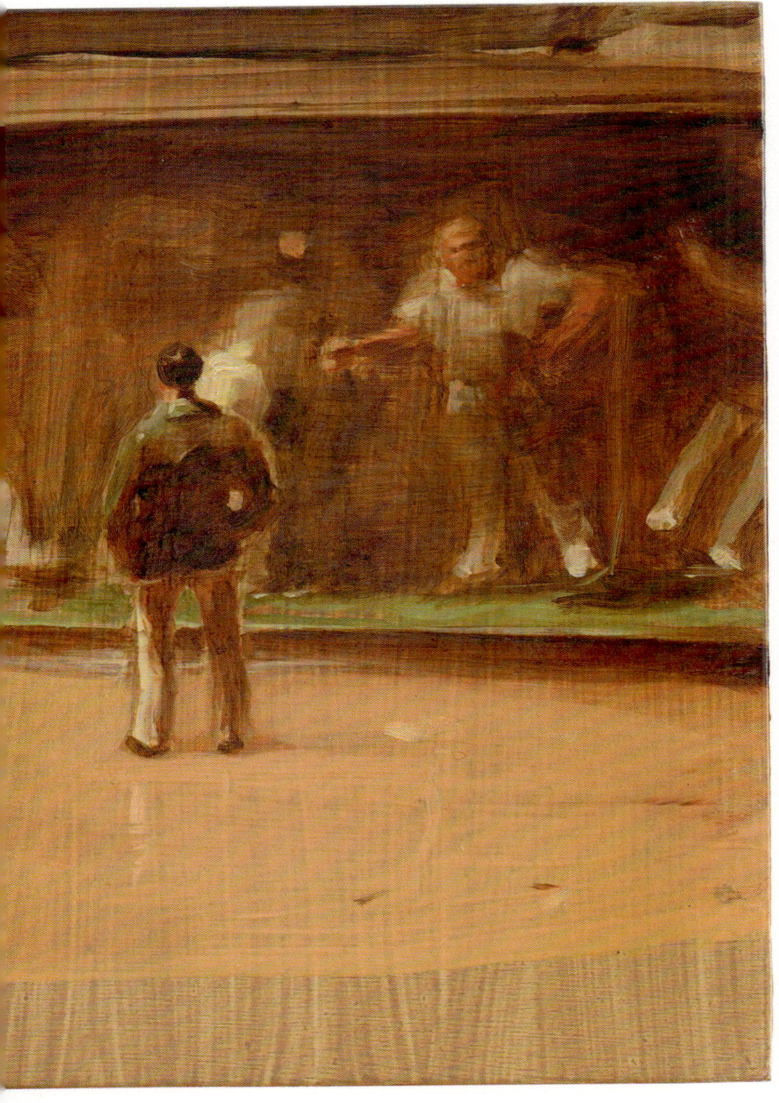

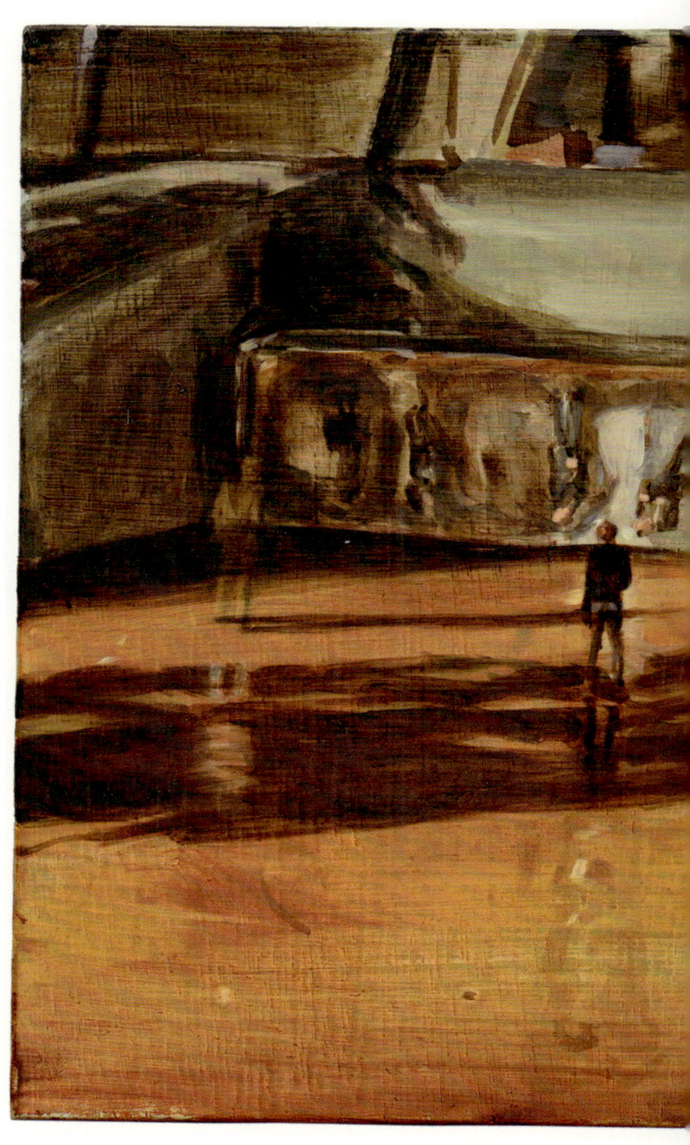

  Five Writers (Design for a Sculpture), 2021

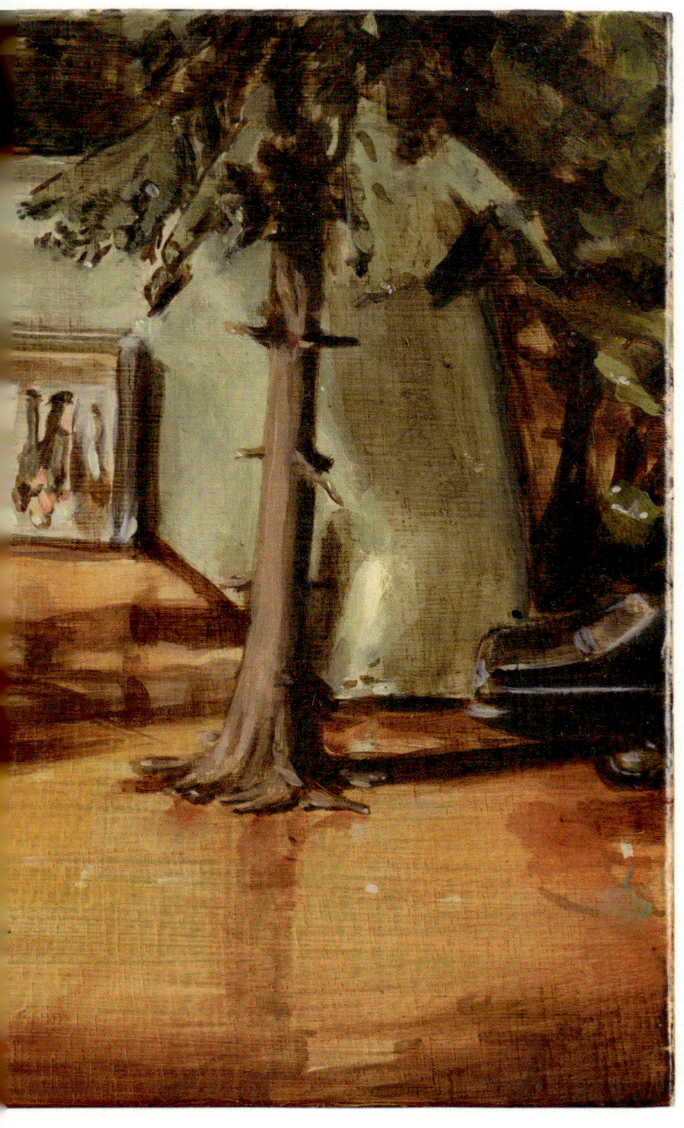

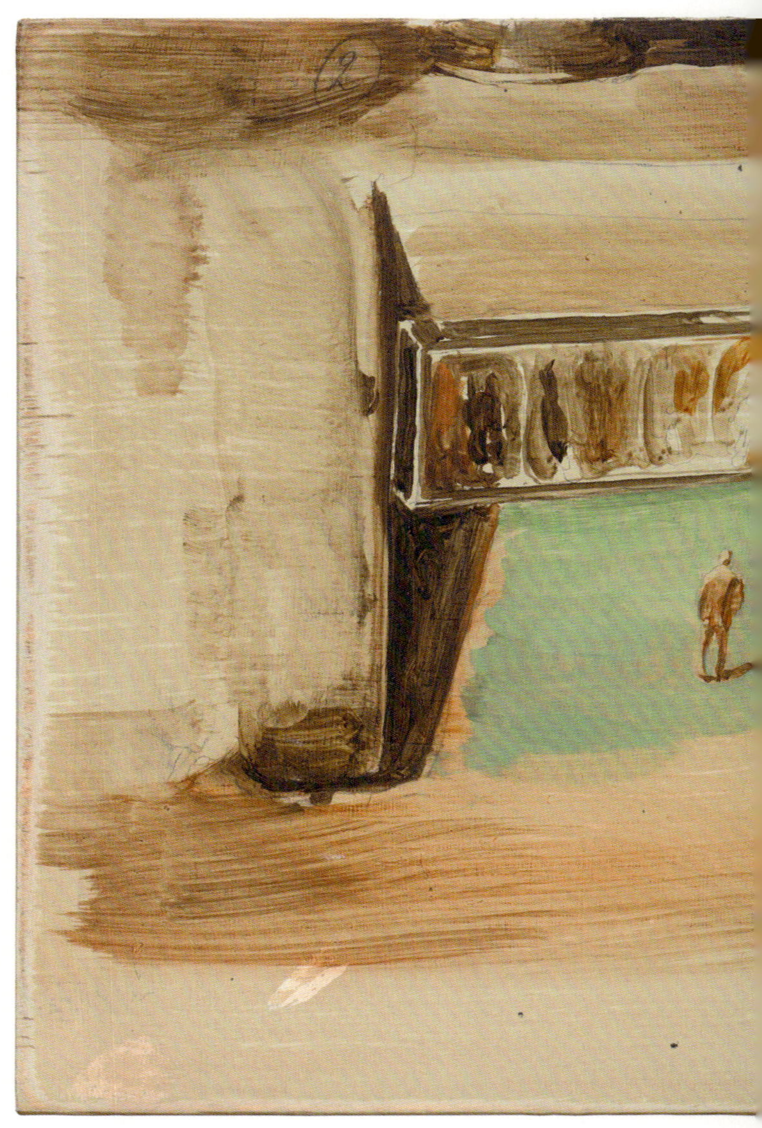

   Five Writers (Design for a Sculpture), 2021

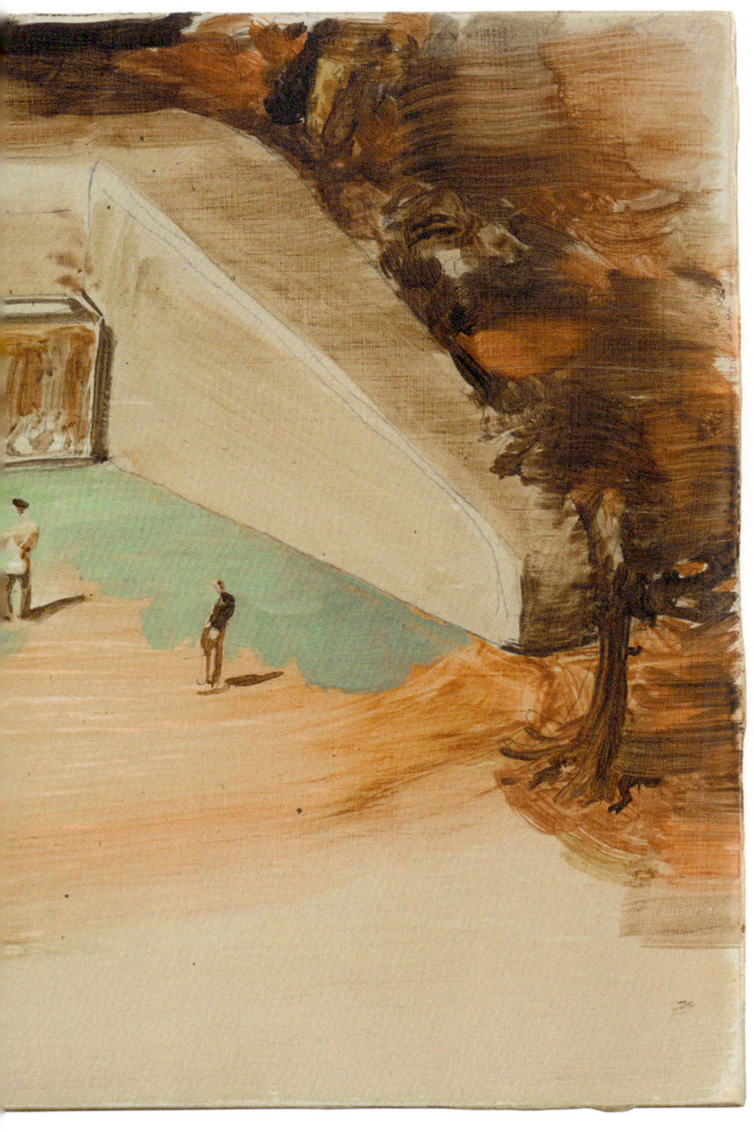

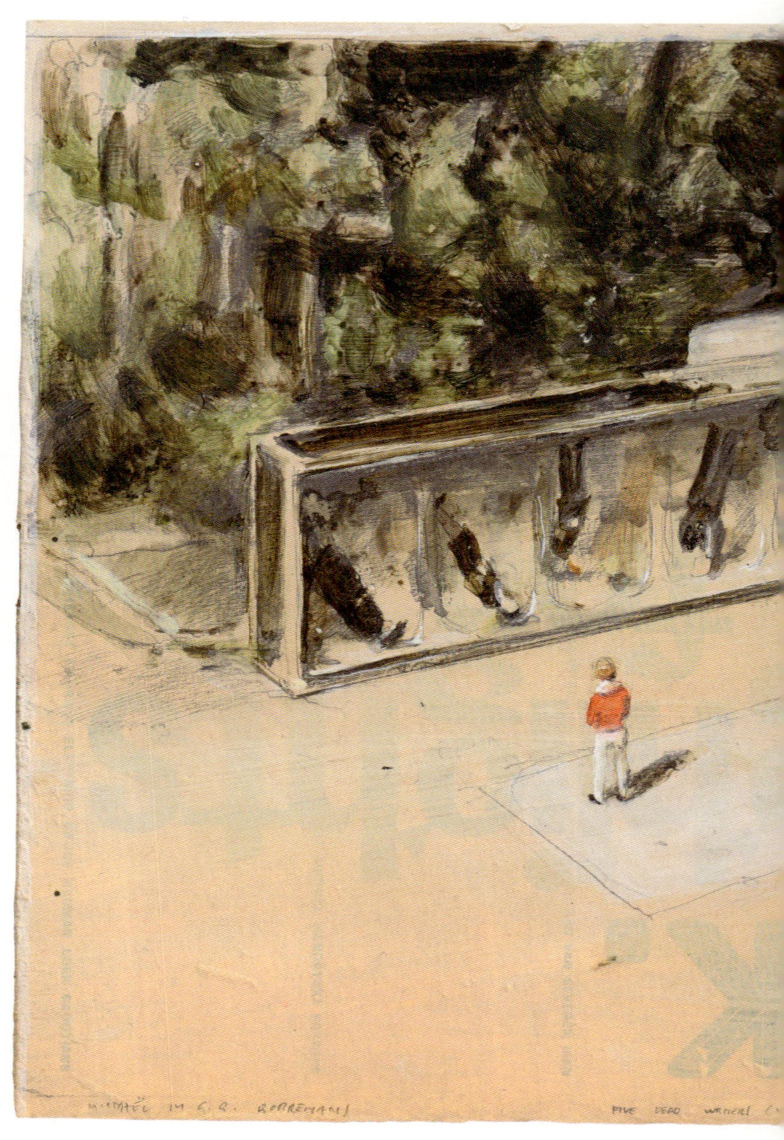

  Five Writers (With Lift for Viewers), 2020

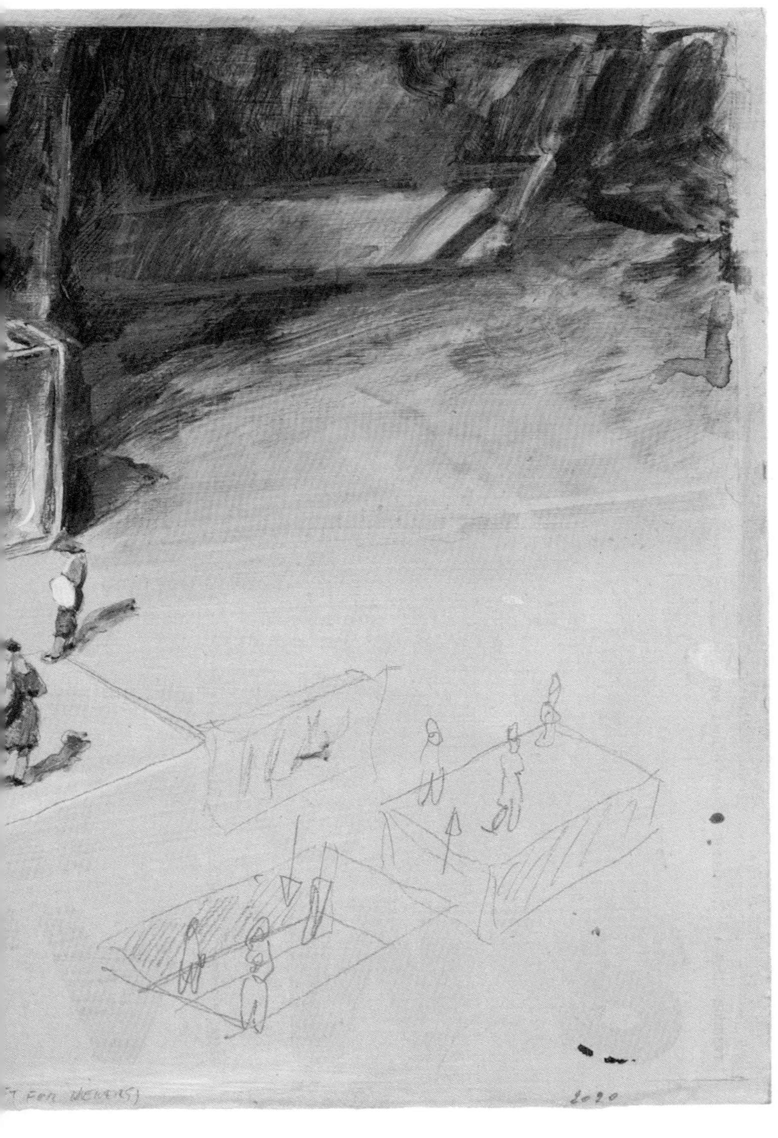
T FOR WEWERS)
2020

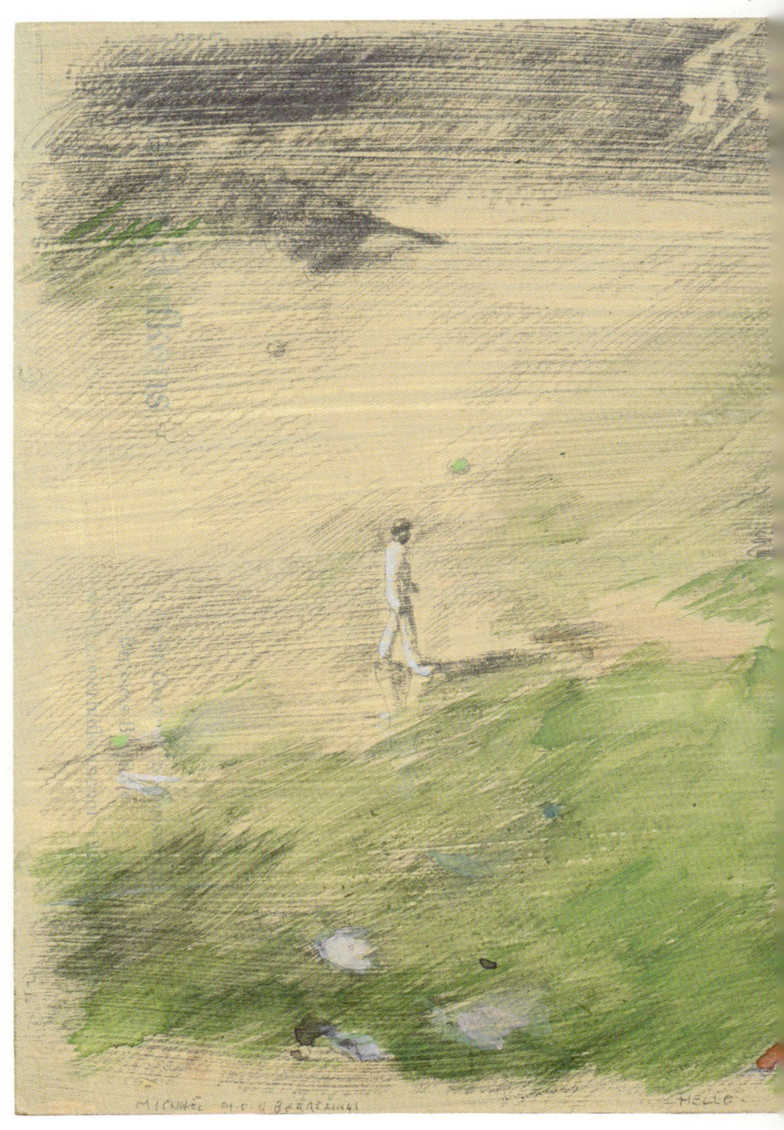

    HELLO (Design for a Sculpture), 2021

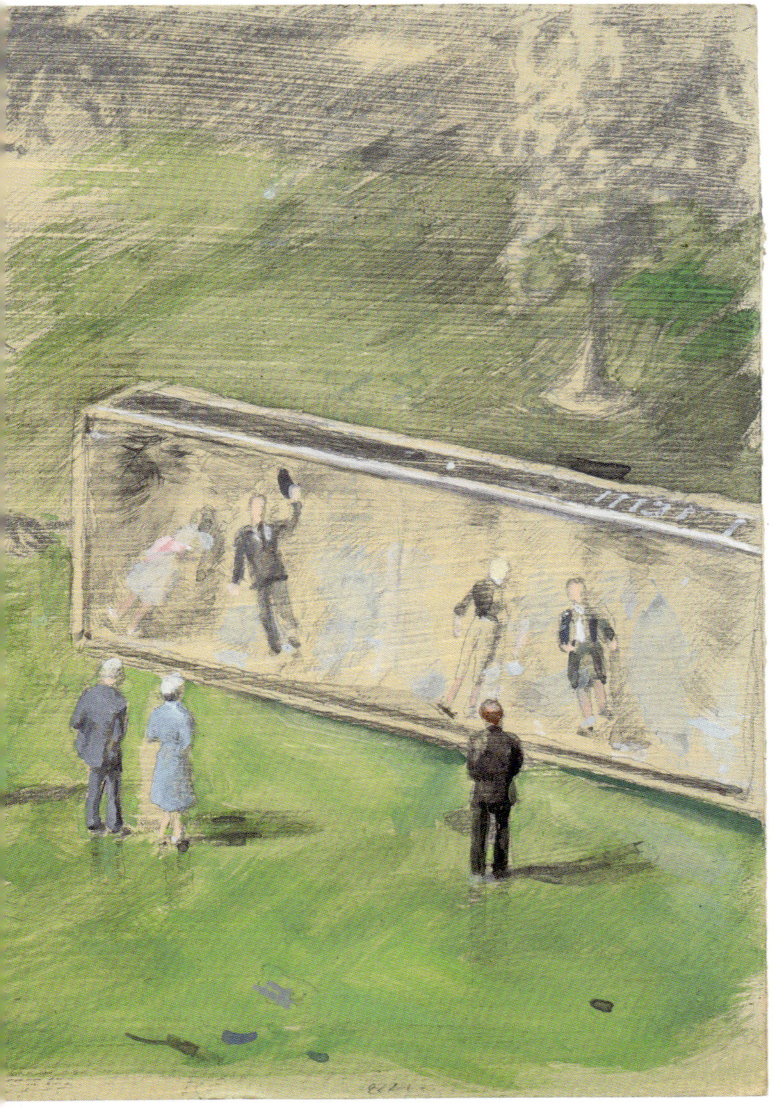

The Acrobat: So-Called Landscapes

"Over-emotion is taboo. I am embarrassed, sometimes, looking at my work and seeing where I have been overly romantic. It is one of the restrictions I give myself. There is a sense of reservation in my work." —Michaël Borremans

Art is just one object with which to fill a vitrine. Mounted butterflies another, cuts of meat or war medals others still. As metaphors, the contents of Borremans's display cases are any or all of the above. It is the vitrine, and not the human, that is the recurring character across *The Acrobat*'s landscape paintings, which really aren't landscapes, deceitful as they are, just as *The Acrobat*'s portraits really aren't portraits. The vitrine has a mystical quality here. Despite the nature surrounding it, the glass remains clean of tree sap, bird droppings, and fingerprints. It is, apparently, a newcomer. Somebody offstage might care devotionally for the structure, perhaps the artist himself.

Relative to its onlookers, the structure is roughly twice their human scale, unearthly in its presence and reminiscent of a toppled monolith from Stanley Kubrick's *2001: A Space Odyssey*. Unlike Kubrick's prop, however, Borremans's object of idolatry does little to arouse emotion from the primates surrounding it. The spectators gaze upon the vitrine and its disturbing contents with the same dispassion they would afford a bowl of oatmeal. If their outfits weren't so very well ironed, you'd think them wicked, punitive, or lacking compassion. But they are an evolved species—the reserved—impervious to fight or flight, and fluent in inoffensive chatter of little consequence, even when faced with the grotesque. Read as if they were figures in an architectural model, or a caricature of gallery goers at an art opening, the onlookers are accusatory. They are, humorously, you and me.

But the paintings that make up *The Acrobat* never propagandize. As in all his work, Borremans disembowels his scenarios of plot or moral. Three titles do indicate at least "five writers," which bullies the viewer into considering a story: A romantic comedy set at a public execution, for example, whose characters are European noncombatants in the ten years following World War II; Alfred Hitchcock's favorite extras from *The Birds*; or spillover crowd from Georges Seurat's *Un dimanche après-midi à l'Île de la Grande Jatte.* Before they can finish the story, the five writers run out of oxygen in their display case.

Borremans says he is embarrassed by any abundance of emotion in his work. "It is one of the restrictions I give myself," he says, to undercut any loss of composure. The works are never sentimental or visibly aggressive. Borremans's art also satirizes embarrassment itself, with exaggerated depictions of politeness. The artist builds a levee against heightened emotionality, and sometimes hopes to see it breached by floods. Notice the distance at which the onlookers gaze at the vitrines, as if the contents might tumble out and crush them. Yes, these are paintings made across two years of a global pandemic, and an allegory of isolation leaps out in a puff of confetti. Then again, Borremans's works have always cautioned against standing too close.

His paintings should come with another warning: Do not take the artist's explanations at face value. Borremans calls this collection of works *Designs for a Sculpture*. The

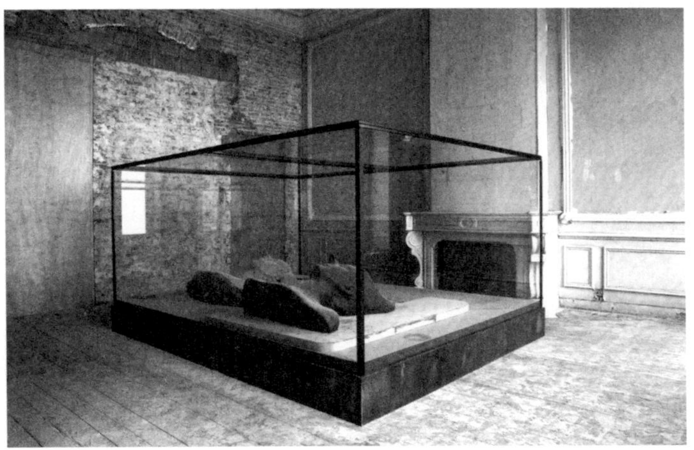

Everything Falls, 2012. Mixed media, 61⅜ × 120 × 91¾ inches | 156 × 305 × 233 cm

same phrase is written into the paintings' titles and onto some of their backgrounds. One would not be faulted, therefore, for believing Borremans and understanding these works as simply drafts for a future project.

Borremans's existing sculptures do offer a logical space for these proposals to fill. *The Acrobat*'s concepts are related to *Rosa* (2017), a large-scale sculpture in the snowy mountains of Gstaad, Switzerland, that depicts a hooded human figure (reminiscent of the artist's *Black Mould* figures from 2014 to 2016) planted headfirst in the snow, bare feet bowing above the bystander. The three *Five Writers* works (2020–2021; pp. 16–21) and *HELLO (Design for a Sculpture)* (2021; pp. 22–23) breathe that same air—or rather eat the same soil—except their hostages are allowed their evening wear, are perhaps even coerced into wearing it. In addition, Borremans's 2012 sculpture, *Everything Falls* (made of bronze, wood, plastic, steel, dust, "and paint, of course," says the artist), is housed in a glass vitrine. Sculptures occupy our physical reality more so than paintings. "The fact that they are part of our world is a problem for me," says Borremans. "I like sculptures even better when I cannot touch them. As in painting, I like for the medium to mystify the work." Whether as paintings or as realized sculptures, *The Acrobat*'s images can never be entered.

Conceivably, these paintings will one day become sculptures. "It's an ambition," says the artist. But each work is also a closed circuit, finished and final, a self-sustaining planet within Borremans's universe. *The Acrobat*'s landscapes recall Borremans's works from the early 2000s, which similarly play with bizarre and intimidating scales and inject functional architectural models with soft hallucinogens (for example, *The House of Opportunity*, 2004, and *The Greatness of Our Loss*, 2006). Borremans draws a parallel between contrived body language—humans acting "fake"—and, say, a fake tree. What's false is funny. What tries to pass for natural rarely does. In comparison to the aesthetic tautness of *The Acrobat*'s portraits, the landscapes are looser, the artist's hand more cavalier. Borremans has made two works in watercolor and pencil on cardboard (*HELLO* and *Five Writers [With Lift for Viewers]*), giving unexpected material a speaking role. The other works in this group are executed in oil on wood panel. A rhythm change is not atypical for Borremans. The song is still very much his.

That said, surrealism, as a mascot for Borremans's approach, should be fired. It's not up to the job. The surre-

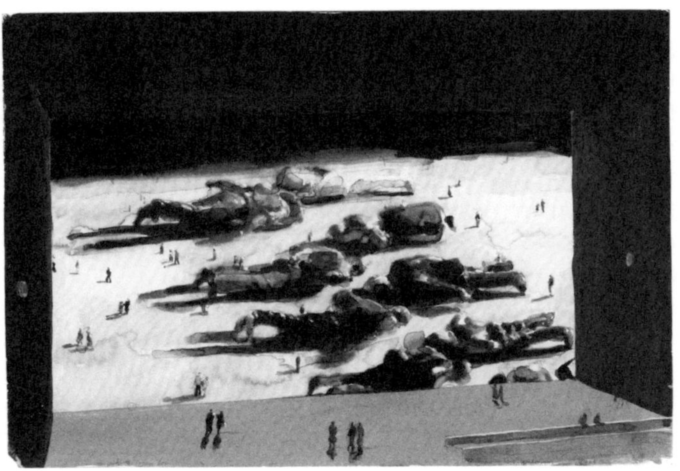

The Greatness of Our Loss, 2006. Pencil, watercolor, and acrylic on paper, 8¼ × 3¾ inches | 21 × 29.6 cm

alists valued automatism, a lack of conscious intent, and they spoke in terms more closely related to intoxication. Borremans, meanwhile, is sober in creating his states of delirium. In a tug of war between shaman and architect, Borremans pulls harder toward architect. Architects carefully measure and implement unconscious desires into their art, but a purely surrealist architecture firm would have too many lawsuits on its hands.

When Borremans engineers the strange, he intends for it to stay upright; for the figure or expectation flipped on its head to stay that way. In this sense, Borremans's sentiments are related more closely perhaps to Dada. They are an intentional response to the world's frightening indifference. They are absurd and playful in defiance of tragedy—a circus built on a burial site. Just look at *Five Writers (With Lift for Viewers)*: Borremans has tenderly placed his viewers on a moving platform without any safety railings, intending to lower them underground as if in a casket, perhaps into Dante's Inferno, or the artist's own divine comedy. The living go under, while their antonym (the vitrine's contents) is forced to stay above ground. When realized, Borremans's lift will certainly be functional. The artist is not interested in idle decoration or metaphor without proper levers of operation.

Two of the *Five Writers* landscapes feature a prominent piece of infrastructure: a concrete culvert—which could be part of an abandoned bridge or another generic artifact

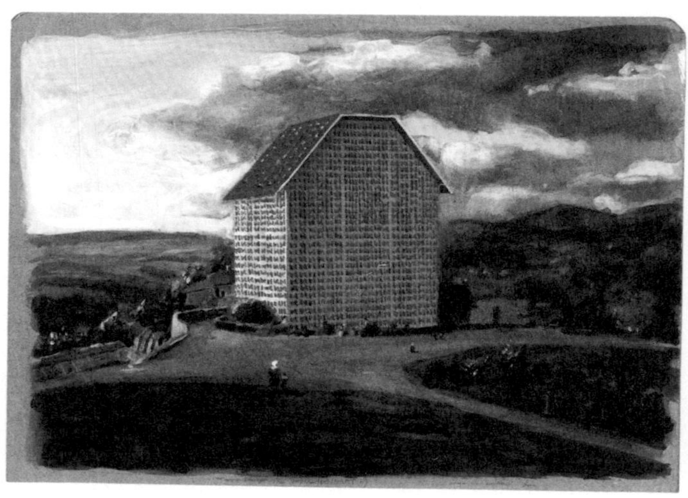

The House of Opportunity, 2004. Pencil, watercolor, and gouache on cardboard,
7 × 9⅞ inches | 18 × 25 cm

of civilization—in the process of being swallowed by the environment. These paintings have the quality of a warm nature hike where occasional signs caution of undetonated mines. One would like to brush such cruelty off from beauty, but one would also like to keep one's remaining limbs intact.

In conversation, Borremans informally refers to these works as "the pagoda drawings." As an architectural type— tall, tiered, and towering—the traditional pagoda itself, built to enshrine the dead, is not visible in these works. What is visible: the thick, sticky air of sacred structures that house human remains. The shape and monumentality of the culvert evokes ancient architecture of a different sort, in particular the Mortuary Temple of Hatshepsut, in which the pharaoh is entombed. Borremans breeds this ancient mortuary with modernist architecture, in the vein of a Mies van der Rohe, and creates a mausoleum fit for today's domestic and dapper. Without intervention from the living, death is otherwise unsightly and impolite. This body of work is a devious pun about paying one's respects.

And here is where Borremans becomes irritated by the weight of painting and meaning, so he teases his heavy medium with light references to conceptual art. One thinks of Marcel Duchamp's *The Bride Stripped Bare by Her Bachelors, Even (The Large Glass)* (1915–1923)—composed painstakingly of materials such as dust (as in *Everything Falls*) and lead wire, which are sandwiched between two panes of glass measuring roughly nine by six feet. Duchamp attempted to encase and preserve something routine and funny. The glass ultimately cracked. Duchamp, being Duchamp, called the shattered glass an improvement upon the work. Borremans, meanwhile, finds some bodies in the dark, dusts them off, and preserves them in shatterproof oil, watercolor, and pencil. His works also contain a ready allusion to Damien Hirst's encased and preserved animal bodies, such as the tiger shark of *The Physical Impossibility of Death in the Mind of Someone Living* (1991). But formaldehyde leaks, Borremans reminds us, while milk is wholesome and calcium keeps bones from rapid decay (see *Milk [or The Acrobat] [Design for a Sculpture]*, 2021; pp. 10–11).

In the 1970s, Primo Levi published a short story called "Tantalio" ("The Magic Paint"), in which a paint manufacturer produces "a paint that provided protection from misfortune." One test subject, painted head to toe in the magic substance, spends four hours of a Friday under a ladder in the company of thirteen black cats, all without incident. After many more favorable results, the paint is applied to the glasses of a poor nobody who has spent his entire life followed by misfortune. He is thought to be an unwitting possessor of the evil eye. After his glasses are covered with the magic paint and allowed to dry, he puts them on and drops dead—his unlucky gaze reflected back at him.

Borremans's paint is likewise magic. The artist welcomes the world's unlucky black cats, ladders, witches, superstitions, and dark spirits. He offers them happy asylum from a condemnatory world. Look closely at what the artist has penciled onto the work *Five Writers (With Lift for Viewers)*, however. He has written: "Five *Dead* Writers." Borremans knows that his paint is as magical as it is lethal.

The Acrobat: So-Called Portraits

"I refuse to see art in a timeline."

"They may be fictional figures, but they are real to me."
—Michaël Borremans

Backstage of a *commedia dell'arte* play might look something like this: a cast of characters descending from a state of suspended disbelief—or crashing, in the proverbial sense. The era in which their performance takes place, whether the seventeenth century or our current epoch of precision diagnostics, is unimportant. In each painting, Borremans compresses chronology into a single frame and sweeps away the rubble of confusion. In terms of both composition and psychology, he unifies disorientation. The artist is a consensus builder between the genteel and the anarchic.

The Acrobat's (so-called) portraits initially register as cohesive and sane, anchored by familiar symbols, such as the human face and torso, and the tranquilized postures of religious icons. Let's first examine these characters sympathetically, as if they were patients brought to a contemporary physician's office, where today's take on the Hippocratic oath forbids exorcisms and bloodletting.

The patients exhibit signs of exhaustion and irritation. They seem to have abruptly turned their faces off following exaggeration and an expulsion of energy. Their bodies slouch in incomplete stages of costume and makeup removal. They are "centaurs"—half boring civilian, half fictional beast. Those wearing heavy costumes should be hot to the touch, but they do not grant physical examination. They could, indeed, be bloodless and dead cold. Layers of paint feel like old sweat that ought to be scrubbed from bodies and outfits. Nostalgia emanates from these paintings: a Proustian phantom scent of mildew and spilled alcohol, bodies and bacteria. This particular decay is casually depressing and vaguely seductive.

In the old traveling theater, characters traditionally represent types, such as lovers and those who keep them apart, servants, the wealthy, the fools, and so on. *The Acrobat*'s painted costumes fail to identify their subjects as any of the above. The titles mystify: *The Acrobat*, *The Apprentice*, *The Commuter*, *The Cutter*, *The Double*, *The Pilot*, *The Racer*, *The Witch*. Like the paintings themselves, the titles are a hazy amalgam of the present (*pilot*) and timeless (*witch*), fantastical and ordinary, dangerous and funny, charmed and cursed. These references all dwell in the same enchanted forest, declaring neutrality.

More literally, the titles—including the overarching title for this body of work, *The Acrobat*—suggest motion, occupation, and performance. The images, meanwhile, are still. Their subjects appear to be idling. One way to understand their postures and expressions is as evidence of intense concentration; as a meditation prior to an adrenalized feat or the *petite mort* of its completion. But such tidy narratives are preposterous, given the emotional disorder of Borremans's work. When the mind tries to rationalize, and the eyes and brain try to compromise, the artist's false flags have gotten the best of them.

For the person who breezes past titles, ignores museum didactics, and sees a collection of images as purely visual, it is reasonable to understand *The Acrobat* as portraits of automatons in the *off* mode. This sort of scene is often referred to as "the uncanny" in Borremans's work. The artist's expressionistic deepfake is his subjective, sensitive ability to depict human life while simultaneously suggesting the absence of a beating heart. "I do not paint portraits," Borremans says. If not "portraits," then what? *Nature morte*?

Close inspection reveals important differences between related characters. The figure in the headlining *Acrobat* (2021; p. 47) has a shadow behind the right shoulder. The other characters do not. They occupy different architectures or different storage units. They stand at different markers on the stage, relative to the spotlight. Or perhaps they occupy different planets and live under different suns. Who is the figure in *The Double* (2022; p. 51)? A body double or a clone? Is this body up against a wall or lying still on a hardwood floor, fallen, unconscious? When the viewer reaches *The Double*, the effect is physically dizzying, as if from moving one's head too quickly. Another anomaly: *The Apprentice* (2022; p. 43) comes close to catching the viewer's eye. This is strange not just in this collection but in Borremans's entire oeuvre. One can call the expressions he paints aloof, but not confrontational. It is more common to see a back turned to you, such as the figure's in *The Commuter II* (2022; p. 55), than to catch an eye. The artist has entered a different psychological dimension here. *The Apprentice* is on the border of picking a fight.

Of the "portraits," *The Witch* (2022; p. 45) is the most obvious visual misfit. Folklorically, witches are most often female. Although Borremans removes most indications of sex in this group of works, the witch here might be a young man, twentysomething, wearing a generic contemporary outfit, without any makeup. He is the most terrestrial of the characters, average in his build and trappings, but he carries the most otherworldly designation. The painting mummifies him in a pose reminiscent of a patron saint.

When Kazimir Malevich, in the 1930s, abandoned abstractionism under duress and made figurative portraits, including a self-portrait, he cast some figures in similarly pious poses. These later works are commonly interpreted unironically, as an about-face from abstraction to representation. But the figures and gestures easily communicate subversion. *Pray to the artist for good harvest.* Borremans's *Witch* also sparks a psychological war between sincerity and irony. It is unlikely that Borremans is directly quoting Malevich, but his work is so exhilaratingly permeable that disparate references easily pass through and live within it comfortably. The artist revels in unexpected interpretations. (Malevich, by the way, also painted faceless, masked, and hooded figures.)

As stock characters, witches are shapeshifters and mediums who live outside of time, traveling between the living and the dead. The witch can heal, curse, or taunt and, as a symbol, is currently enjoying a revival—a symptom of our uncertain times. The supernatural is fun. It lets us think we have control over ourselves, others, the future. Borremans's witch is also fun, an unlikely guide for the other figures through periods of transformation. While the other characters are all mid-metamorphosis (costumes and makeup half-baked), the witch is the only one either fully undisguised or seamlessly incognito: a spy, a harmless backstage intern, or the main puppeteer.

This is a funny comment on the artist's role, questioning whether he has control over his paintings or is at their mercy. Are they his vision, or is he theirs? Seen a different way, the characters are perhaps towering above the artist, looking down at him. Many of them have cast their gaze downward.

Borremans says that, for the first time in his work, *The Acrobat*'s portraits allow the viewer to "feel the fiction." One should be used to such mysterious statements from the artist by now, but this comment seems particularly suspicious. Fiction, or at least its blood relative, seems integral to all of Borremans's works.

The difference is subtle. In this new body of work, in contrast to his earlier portraits, Borremans has constructed a world in which the cement is still wet, and half the light bulbs are broken. He typically presents airtight illusions and hermetic fantasies. This time, he shows us a fantasy after last call. The lights have come on and we suddenly see the poor construction of the costumes and the misaligned seams. Borremans paints the sloppy exquisitely, as if giving his loving attention to the rejects and understudies of earlier work.

At the opening of his exhibition *Fire from the Sun*, at David Zwirner, Hong Kong, in 2018, Borremans noted that people used broad adjectives to compliment the work but that few said aloud what they actually saw. Whatever aphorisms or metaphors visitors invoked, few acknowledged that, broadly, the paintings show cherubs tearing into human limbs: angelic baby cannibals. In a different anecdote, Borremans recalled an unforeseen reaction to his painting *Red Hand, Green Hand* (2010) in Budapest in 2011. The image was widely understood as a symbol of Hungary's political circumstances and flown on a large banner promoting the show. When Borremans asked why this was the case, the curator said that the painting explains "the situation in the country we live in. It shows two contrasting hands, but they come from the same body."

This demonstrates Borremans's very original dilemma. Whereas artists typically "complain" that the public doesn't understand their abstraction and wants only to see "something," Borremans finds that his audience can more readily talk of his work as abstraction rather than in concrete terms.

The Acrobat is also likely to circulate broad adjectives among its viewers: *beautiful, delicate, haunting*. Will it feel awkward for a visitor to comment on the characters' ripped clothing and dejected bodies? Some of the figures appear annoyed by the very idea of beauty. Others appear tired. The temperament in this body of work is something different. It is nervous. Borremans says that in comparison to his other works, "*The Acrobat* has a different psychological depth."

But back to broad adjectives. In tandem with menacing, Borremans's work is also largely regarded as romantic. It is a term used by critics and the artist alike. Though meant, in most cases, to indicate opposition in his paintings (repulsion versus attraction), the romantic does not fight other forces in Borremans's work but is instead their willing collaborator. When Borremans uses the term, he intends it with full paradox.

In *The Roots of Romanticism*, Isaiah Berlin's brilliant analysis of Romanticism, the author describes the artistic movement, snaking from the eighteenth through the nineteenth century, as "an attempt to impose an aesthetic model upon reality, to say that everything should obey the rules of art." Later, Berlin writes, the Romantics were "hoist with their own petard. Aiming at one thing, they produced, fortunately for us all, almost the exact opposite."

The Acrobat rings with that same duality. The paintings refuse to obey the rules Borremans imposes upon them. They stage a coup against the artist's aesthetic model, as compared to his earlier works. The artist, consciously or not, at once produces *his* work and its opposite. And the result is mesmerizing, fortunately for us all.

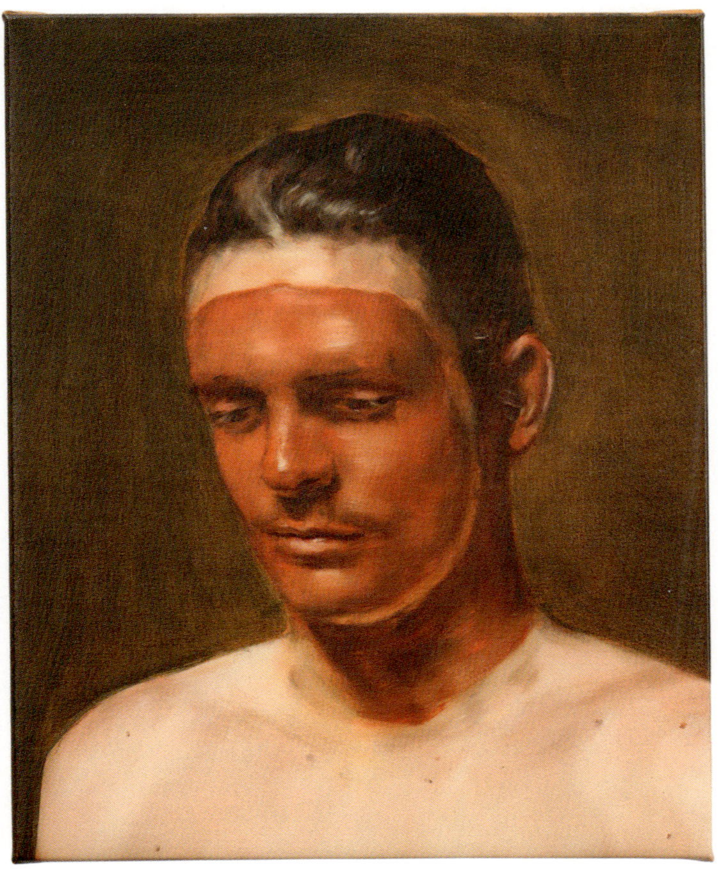

    The Apprentice, 2022

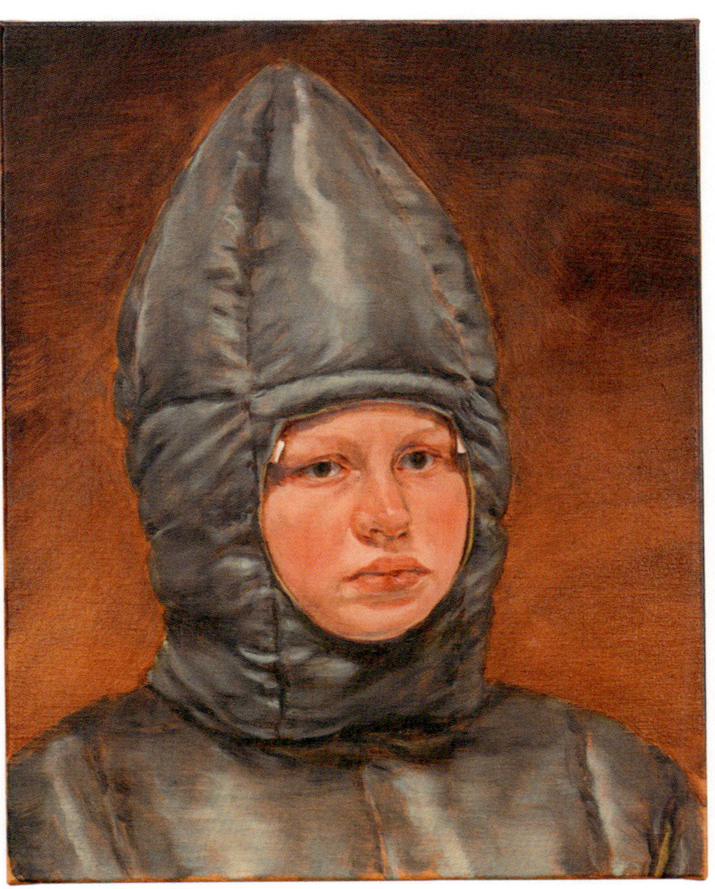

The Witch, 2022

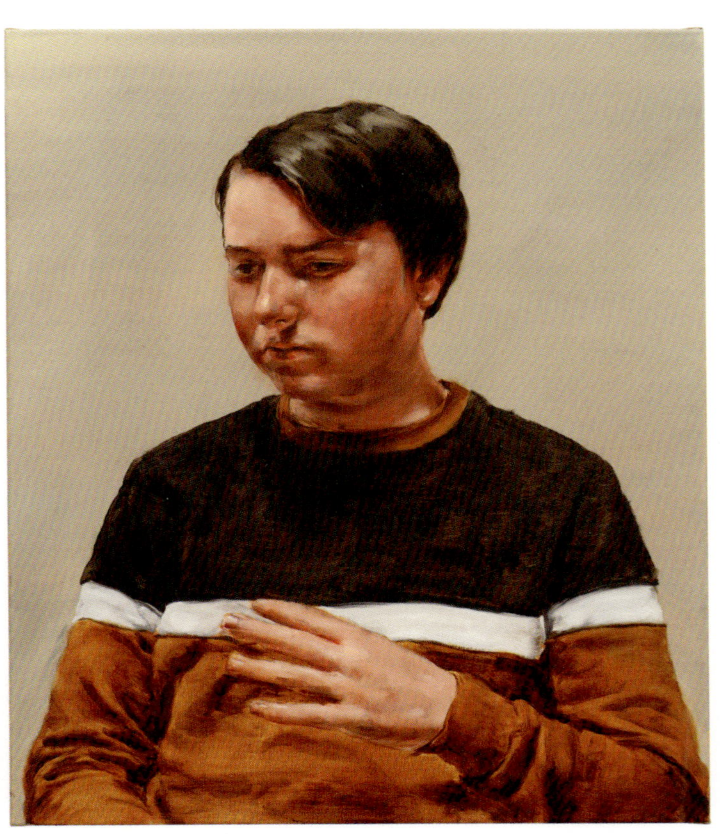

The Acrobat, 2021

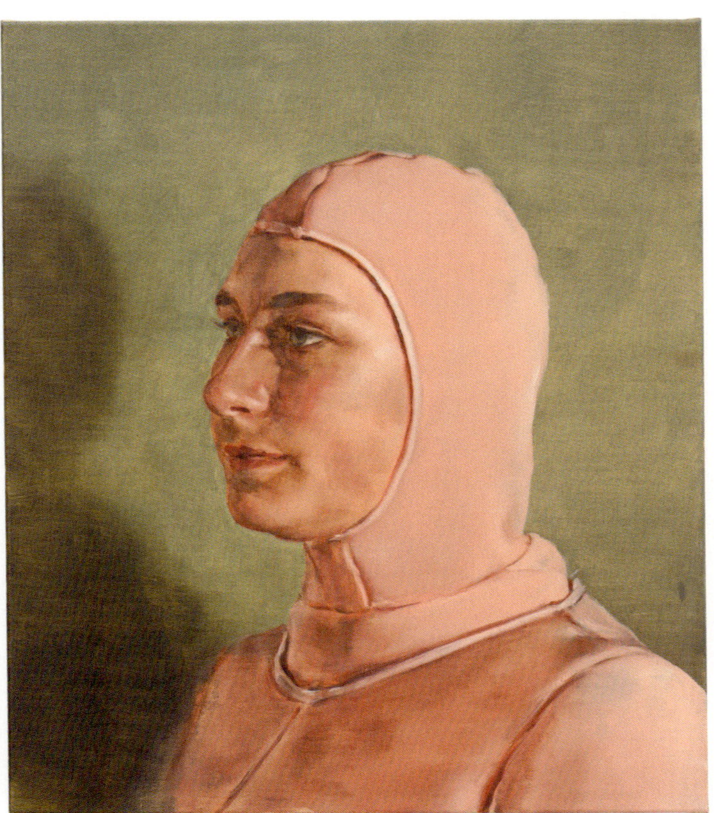

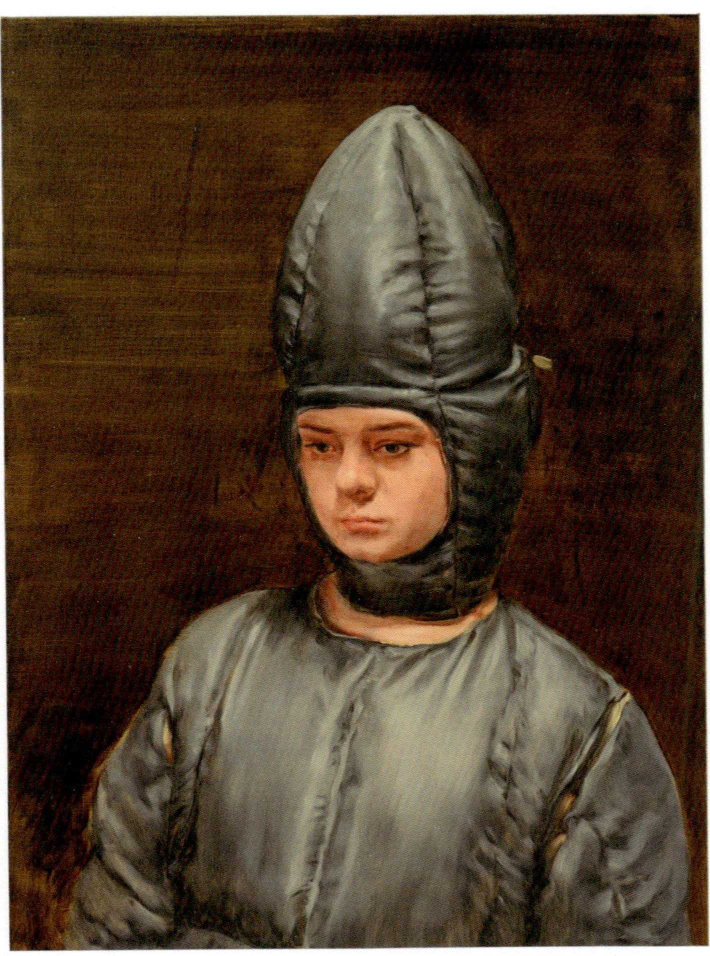

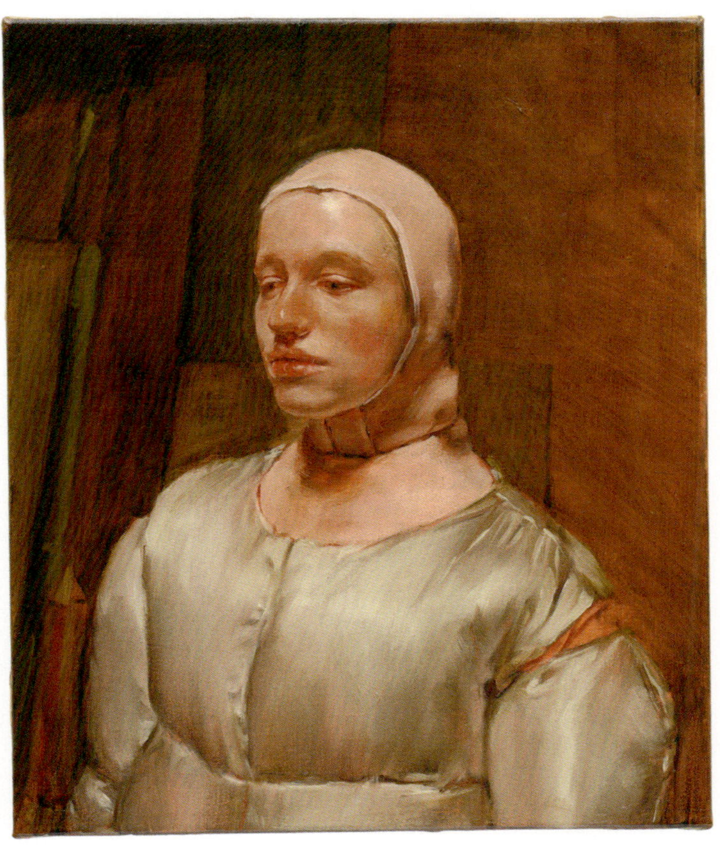

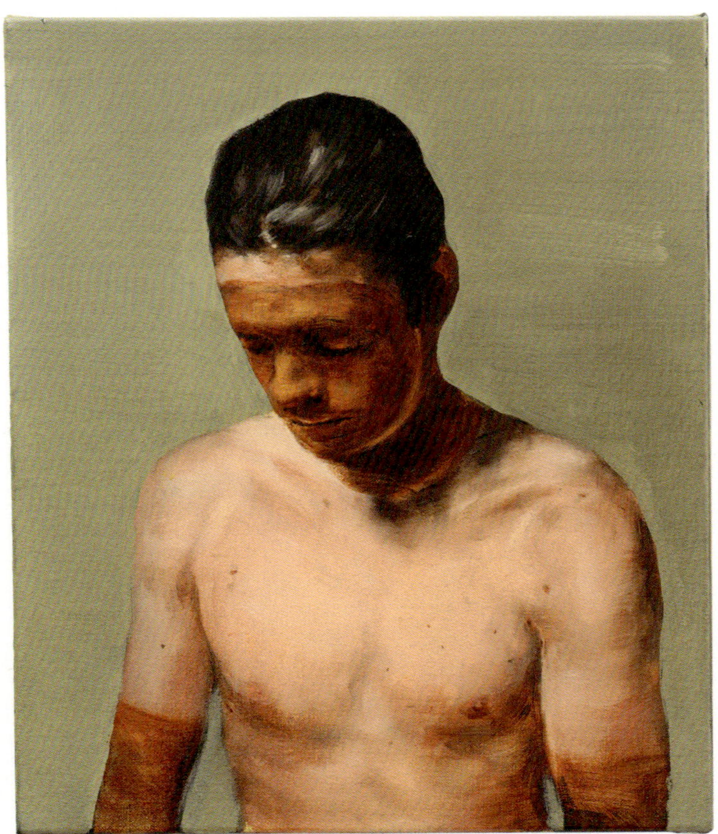

    The Commuter II, 2022

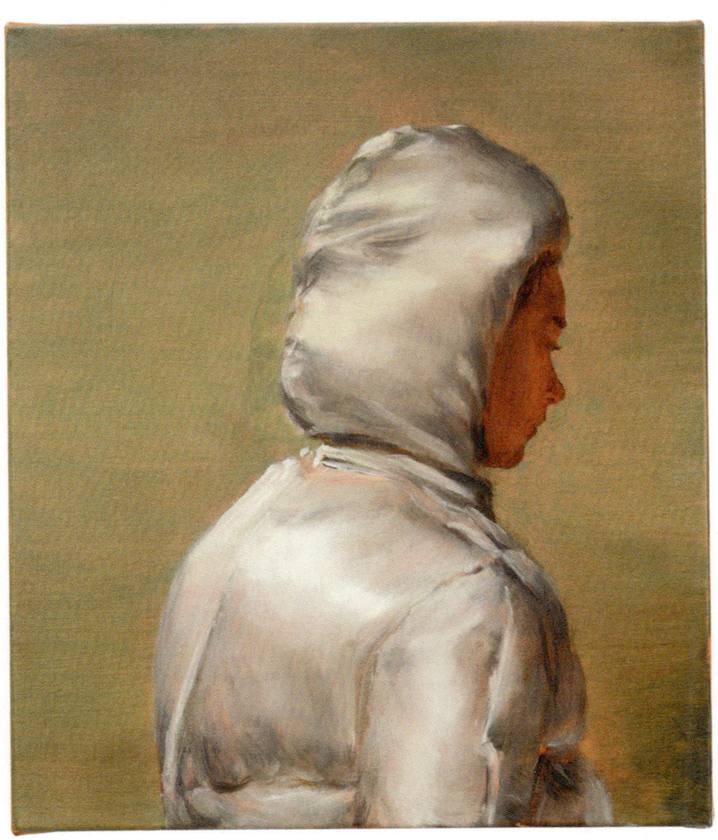

The Acrobat Looks Down from the Tightrope:
An Aerial View

Hooked up to an electrocardiogram, a painting by Borremans betrays its calm outward appearance—internally, the work is adrenalized and palpitating. Here, "work" is a verb that belongs to both artist and artwork. The painting labors to preserve its composure as the artist applies stress on it. He never backs off. While some of Borremans's subjects suggest the lack of a pulse, the same is never true of the painting itself. Its energy could jump-start a dead car.

When explaining what makes an artwork moving, our available vocabulary crumbles and gets stuck in the teeth. For greater ease, these conversations shape themselves into comparisons. This art feels like that art; this artist is similar to that artist. The framework often falls short. It's true, for example, that Borremans cites Édouard Manet as an important artist for him, but how that manifests technically or thematically is elusive. This source of inspiration does not account for Borremans's individual sensitivity to line, shadow, emotion, and gallows humor. It amounts to telling a dog how much it looks like its owners. In affectionate proximity, members of different species can start to resemble one another, as might two artworks placed next to each other, but a surgeon would never mistake one for the other on an operating table. Their guts are different, so are their hearts.

Borremans also speaks with veneration about Johannes Vermeer and Jean-Baptiste-Siméon Chardin, but they are not like Borremans, nor are they like each other, aside from both probably being Scorpios. To say the artists share a sentiment rather than aesthetic is as vague as any astrological generality, but fun nonetheless. Let's go for it. Borremans's work pipes in the mustiness and suffocation of Vermeer's domestic settings. Vermeer's subjects look to the viewer with pleading eyes despite their composure. Borremans's subjects look beyond the viewer but communicate their imprisonment with similar delicacy.

Chardin paints with the irony of a jovial depressive, and his affinity for the odd—including memorable hats and the awkward poses of dead animals—as well as for solitary people doing lonesome things (blowing bubbles, stacking cards), appeals to Borremans. The artists show sympathy toward discomfiture. "I'm not interested in Chardin's technique, but his attitude," says Borremans. "His work evolved the still life as a genre. He did something transcendent and reflective." If Chardin and Borremans were to review headshots of art models together, they would throw out anyone who euphemistically makes love to the camera and—in seeking to transcend and reflect—keep the "un-naturals" instead.

Borremans's work is unlike that of Hieronymus Bosch, yet one can imagine the artists sharing visions of hell over a beer. If considered as panels of an altarpiece, *The Acrobat*'s landscapes are a garden of earthly delights—those delights include voyeurism—and its portraits are the Last Judgment, or whatever happens after curtain call in paradise. Borremans's nude figures, such as those in *The Racer*, *The Cutter*, and the older works *The Nude* (2010) and *The Devil's Dress* (2011), commune with the unbroken but resigned bodies of Bosch's Eve and the condemned everyman. Borremans maintains the integrity of the human body, no matter how mangled its soul. The artist uses his paint as embalming fluid. His figures are not allowed external breakdowns or rudimentary humiliations, and his Eden is denied a libido. Instead of breeding his humans in transparent orbs, as did Bosch when evoking a fetus in utero, Borremans plants his figures in an incubator (*The Acrobat*'s vitrine) to either contradict or simulate nature's organic processes.

Borremans never paints grotesque demons, though he implies psychological ones. Seen up close, *The Acrobat*'s portraits are intermediaries of fright or fantasy, but their hearts aren't in it. Partially scrubbed of makeup and ashes, one suspects the figures of playacting, of going through the motions of disturbance. Their unfinished costumes contrast against the tailored suits worn by both the onlookers and looked-upon in the landscapes. They further contrast the neat human bodies they conceal. These demons are a bad fit. *The Acrobat*'s subjects are pretending. They are engaged in a damnation dress-up.

The twentieth-century literary theorist Mikhail Bakhtin wrote of the medieval carnival and the carnivalesque as a later artistic technique. He described carnival as a sanctioned period of subversion, in which to freely upend the hierarchies and codes of society. Borremans sets a stage of carnival through references to medieval dress and posture, allusions to performance, and confusion of societal cues (particularly in the landscapes). Beyond representing carnival, however, the artist participates in it.

In *Rabelais and His World*, Bakhtin writes: "The satirist whose laughter is negative places himself above the object of his mockery, he is opposed to it. . . . The people's ambivalent laughter, on the other hand, expresses the point of view of the whole world; he who is laughing also belongs to it." The artist is laughing. He allows his viewers to do the same. Borremans's works are funny, but not satire, as they do not necessarily oppose or denigrate their figures and situations. His paintings are no more nonsensical than reality itself. Perhaps the many texts asserting that Borremans "creates his own worlds" miss the joke. He re-creates our world in his own way. Like literature's most memorable passages, Borremans's art communicates what we know already but could not say ourselves. Estrangement is a character in his paintings, not their effect. The paintings engage and understand, even empathize. They invite the viewer to the carnival.

In attendance are some notable twentieth-century artists, among them René Magritte and Francis Bacon. One would never mistake Borremans for either, yet his paintings flirt with the debonair bizarreness of Magritte and the clear-eyed introversion of Bacon. The synthesis of Borremans's work is as conceptual as it is aesthetic and chronological.

Magritte's *The Lovers*, for example, completed in 1928, shows two faces cloaked in fabric and sharing a kiss. Borremans's paintings such as *The Driver* (2010) or *Mercy* (2016), depicting faces cloaked in fabric, might evoke *The Lovers*. In Borremans's nonlinear understanding of art, however, Magritte's work could conceivably be referencing his. Art is a conversation that loses track of the era. Cryptic and exciting, each work is a contradictory thought about connection. On one hand, the art denies connection; on the other, it connects with the viewer and with art itself. While Borremans's paintings do not directly quote other artists, they make like-minded wisecracks. The found object on display is the humor, stretched across ages. One need not be an art historian to get in on the joy of it; simply being alive should do it.

Borremans's paintings don't read like a sentence, beginning to end. They invade the psyche like a sudden memory, occupying the entire concept of existence. Borremans does not insert memento mori into his paintings—his paintings go ahead and deny the inevitability of death. The viewer, instead, becomes the memento mori, suddenly conscious of being a walking skeleton. The painting never heeds the warning. It exists in a sanctioned space, in which the rules of human function and habit are suspended. Borremans's blueprints for this space are precise. His compositions are scrupulous, and he has clearly studied how artists before him engineered their ideas. In the same way we wonder about the stability of our existing world, we wonder if Borremans's scenarios might also one day collapse onto themselves, because he has purposefully sabotaged his infrastructures. He may preserve the integrity of the human body, but he leaves the viewer unsure as to whether the ground beneath his figures will hold, whether the stage lights will malfunction, the vitrine glass will break, or the ceiling will crack and let the elements in. Is there a safety net below the acrobat? Borremans leaves the viewer wondering.

The Acrobat, 2021
Oil on canvas
27½ × 23⅝ inches | 70 × 60 cm
    p. 47

The Apprentice, 2022
Oil on canvas
27½ × 23⅝ inches | 70 × 60 cm
    p. 43

The Commuter II, 2022
Oil on canvas
14⅛ × 11¾ inches | 36 × 30 cm
    p. 55

The Cutter, 2022
Oil on canvas
14⅛ × 11¾ inches | 36 × 30 cm
    p. 53

The Double, 2022
Oil on canvas
14¼ × 11¾ inches | 36.2 × 30 cm
    p. 51

Five Writers (Design for a Sculpture), 2021
Oil on wood panel
7⅝ × 9⅝ inches | 19.5 × 24.4 cm
    pp. 16–17

Five Writers (Design for a Sculpture), 2021
Oil on wood panel
6½ × 10 inches | 16.6 × 25.5 cm
    pp. 18–19

Five Writers (With Lift for Viewers), 2020
Graphite and watercolor on cardboard
grounded with oil paint
5⅞ × 8¼ inches | 14.8 × 21 cm
    pp. 20–21

The Fog (Design for a Sculpture), 2021
Oil on wood panel
8⅜ × 12⅛ inches | 21.3 × 30.8 cm
    pp. 14–15

HELLO (Design for a Sculpture), 2021
Graphite and watercolor on cardboard
grounded with oil paint
5⅞ × 8¼ inches | 14.8 × 20.9 cm
    pp. 22–23

Milk (or The Acrobat) (Design for a Sculpture), 2021
Oil on wood panel
6⅜ × 10⅛ inches | 16.1 × 25.8 cm
    pp. 10–11

The Pilot, 2021
Oil on canvas
47¼ × 34⅝ inches | 120 × 88 cm
    p. 49

The Racer, 2022
Oil on canvas
22 × 17¾ inches | 56 × 45 cm
    p. 41

The Witch, 2022
Oil on canvas
27½ × 23⅝ inches | 70 × 60 cm
    p. 45

With Animals, 2021
Oil on wood panel
7⅝ × 9¾ inches | 19.4 × 24.9 cm
    pp. 12–13

Acknowledgments

David Zwirner wishes to thank Michaël Borremans, without whom this exhibition and publication would not have been possible, as well as Hanna Schouwink and Angela Choon for their close collaboration and support. Our deepest thanks are due to Katya Tylevich for her insightful text.

For their work on the exhibition, we are grateful to Rebecca Ashby-Colón, Mary Stuart Baker, Claire Ball, Christie Bianco, Bianca Boragi, Elizabeth Brannan-Williams, Andrea Brignolo, Cristina Covucci, Jacob Daugherty, Kendall Cashmore, Emily Gachot, Tam Jumbala, Susi Kenna, Coco Kim, Demie Kim, Michelle Kim, Britta Nelson, Julia Lukacher, Chris Medina, Tessa Morefield, Clive Murphy, Charlotte Panis, Haley Darya Parsa, Erin Pinover, Chris Rawson, Max Rosenberg, Janna Singer-Baefsky, Elena Soboleva, Virginia Stroh, Alexandra Whitney, Iona Whittaker, Fan Zhong, and Lucas Zwirner.

For their work on the publication, thanks are due to Kim Beirnaert, Doro Globus, Elizabeth Gordon, Jessica Palinski, Molly Stein, and Joey Young.

Michaël Borremans wishes to thank Viktor Besard, Ginger Bogaert, Xenia Borremans, Maxwell De Broeder, Ciska Van Bockstaele, Manon Vander Perre, and Bernadette and Luc Vandercoilden for their collaboration. Special thanks go to Frederik Debuysscher for his studio assistance and Kim Beirnaert for the book's design. Deepest gratitude is owed to Angela Choon, Hanna Schouwink, and Monica and David Zwirner for the support and pleasant collaboration. Special thanks go to Katya Tylevich for her eloquent and smart essay on the work. Very special thanks to my partner, Kaat De Jonghe, for her ongoing loving support and great collaboration.

Published by David Zwirner Books
on the occasion of

Michaël Borremans: The Acrobat
David Zwirner, 525 West 19th Street,
New York
April 28–June 4, 2022

David Zwirner Books
529 West 20th Street, 2nd Floor
New York, New York 10011
+1 212 727 2070
davidzwirnerbooks.com

Design and Production Manager
    Kim Beirnaert
Project Editor
    Elizabeth Gordon
Color Separations
    die Keure, Bruges
Printing
    die Keure, Bruges

Typeface
    Arnhem Pro
Paper
    Focus Book, 90 gsm
    Terraprint Silk, 90 gsm

All photography by Peter Cox, with the
exception of:
p. 27: Dirk Pauwels
p. 30: Courtesy Zeno X Gallery, Antwerp

Collections
pp. 27, 30: S.M.A.K., Stedelijk Museum
voor Actuele Kunst, Ghent
p. 29: Private collection, San Sebastián,
Spain

Distributed in the United States and
Canada by
    Simon & Schuster, Inc.
    1230 Avenue of the Americas
    New York, New York 10020
    simonandschuster.com

Distributed outside the United States
and Canada by
    Thames & Hudson, Ltd.
    181A High Holborn
    London WC1V 7QX
    thamesandhudson.com

ISBN 978-1-64423-083-1
Library of Congress Control Number
    2022904633

Printed in Belgium

Cover: *The Acrobat*, 2021